A Brush With Art

Darren Griffin

Copyright © 2018 Darren Griffin

All rights reserved.

**ISBN-13:
978-1720684404**

**ISBN-10:
1720684405**

DEDICATION

To my wonderful wife Alicia who always believes in me.
To my seven amazing children who are all artists in their own way.

To anyone who has both a dream and a paintbrush.

CONTENTS

Introduction   i

Seascapes   1

Landscapes   19

This and That   33

About the Author   51

INTRODUCTION

Father's Day of 2017 my daughter Kelly gave me an acrylic paint set. This is the third time she had given me a paint set. I used to do paint by numbers but she believed I had the heart of a true painter. I wasn't so certain. With the first set she gave me I painted a piece that I call "Fish Swimming Through Seaweed" because it was of fish swimming through seaweed.

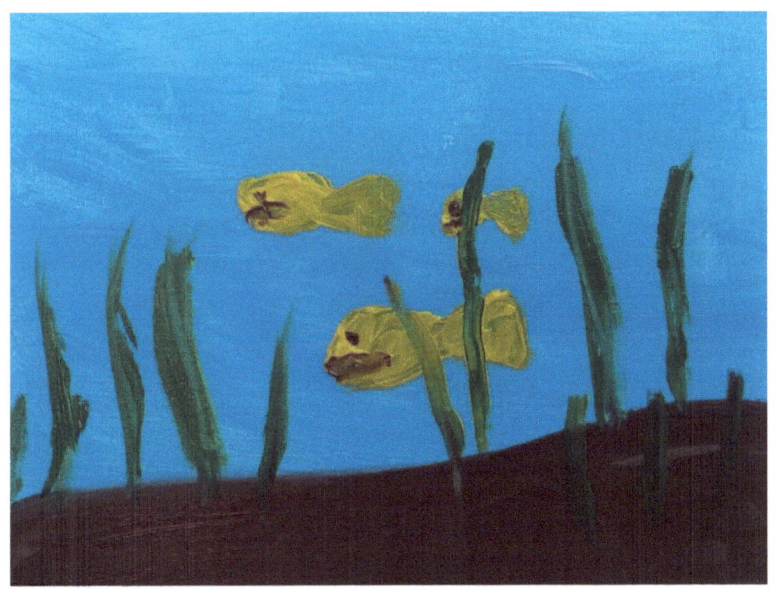

Yeah. I know. Looks like it should be on somebody's fridge. This proved to me that I didn't have the right stuff. Kelly still believed in me though. The second paint set went into a drawer. The third. . . ah, the third.

I had gone through a difficult divorce and was newly remarried and it was as if a switch flipped. I set up an easel, watched tutorials on line and gave it my best shot.

Maybe Kelly was right

Seascapes

One of My First Attempts

I've always had a love of the ocean, so naturally my first few attempts at painting involved the sea. Although this piece has much about it that screams beginner, I've included it because I like the colors and the lighting.

A Brush With Art

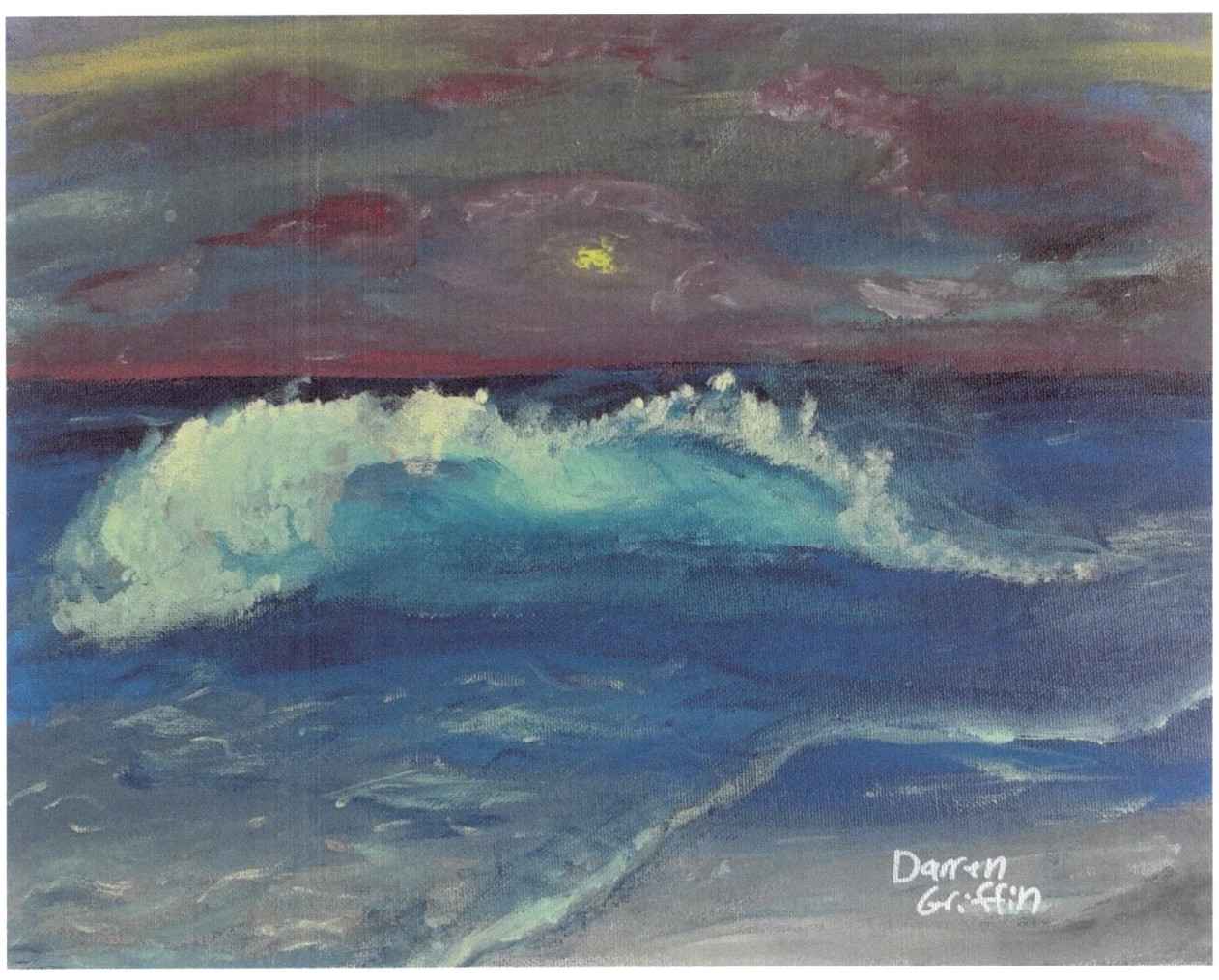

Sunset on Lake Superior

In the summer of 2017 my wife, Alicia, and I drove to Duluth Minnesota for her family reunion. Her brother had a boat on Lake Superior and took us out several times. One evening I took a picture of the sunset and resolved to try and paint it when we returned home. This is the result.

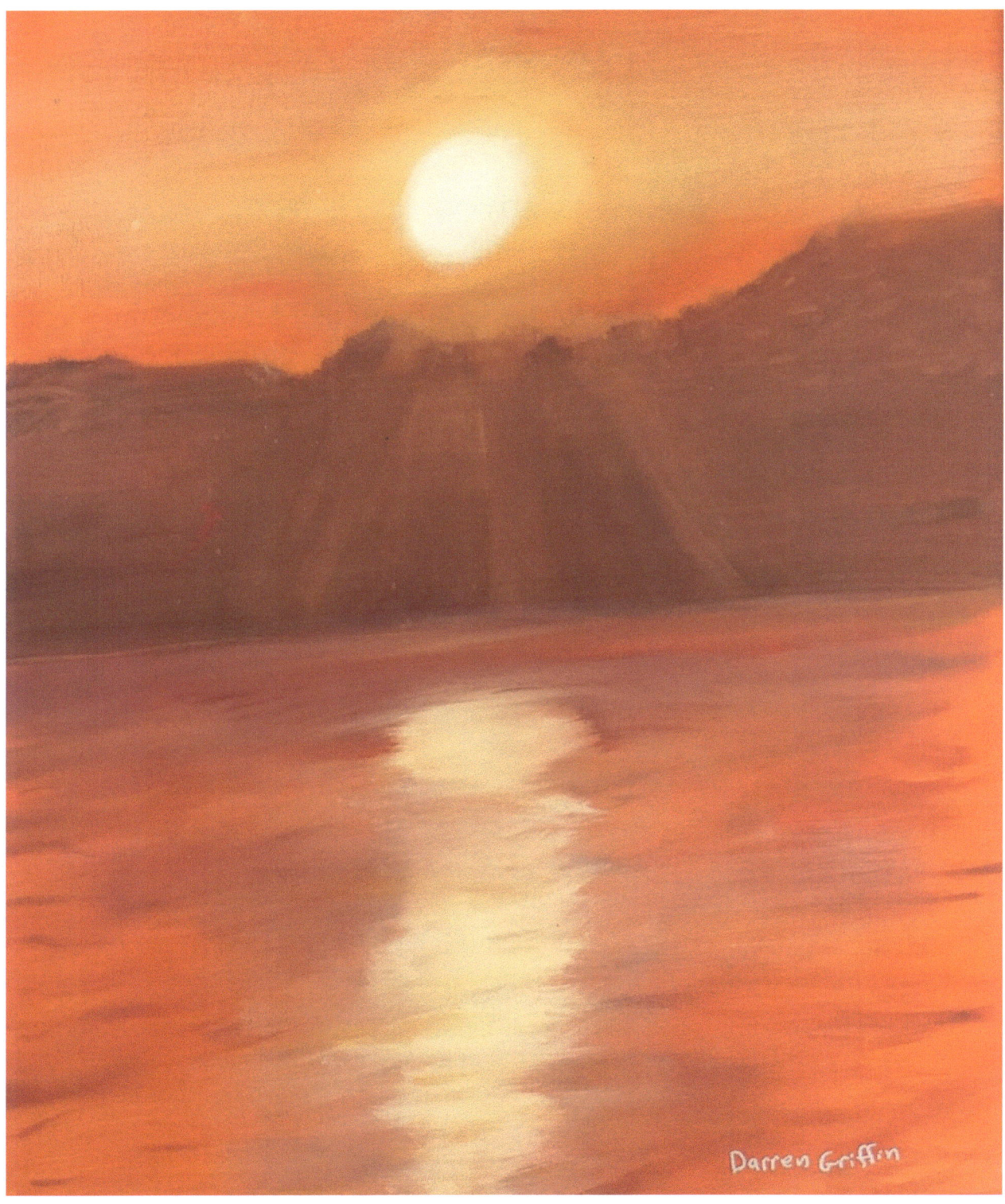

Waves

Waves tend to be a challenge for me. They just don't turn out the way I see them in my head. This piece is an attempt to get the waves right.

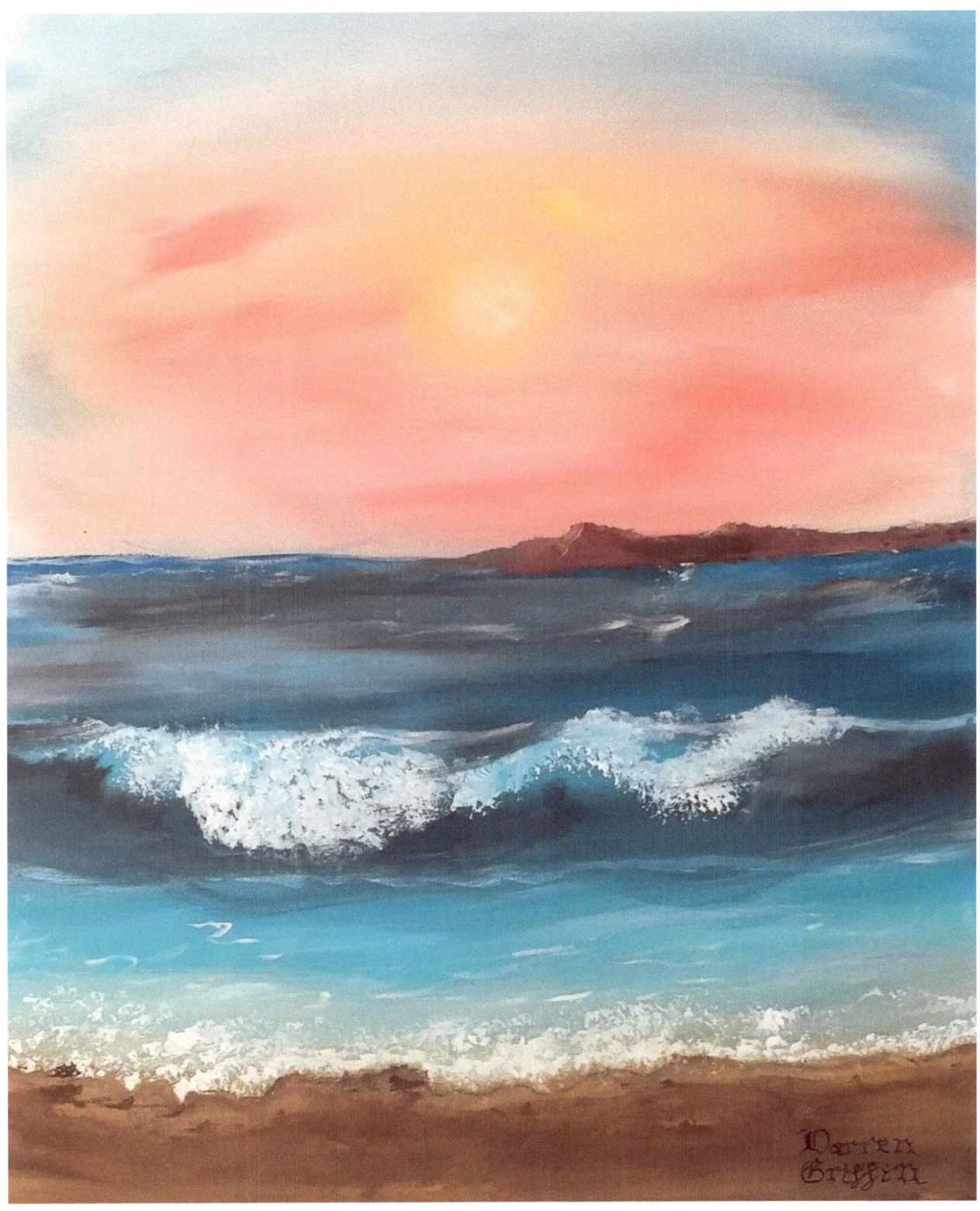

Cliffs

I decided it was time to bring some other objects into my seascapes. I started with a cliff and some rocks and then felt the need for a tree.

I particularly like the texture I got on the cliffs from using a palette knife.

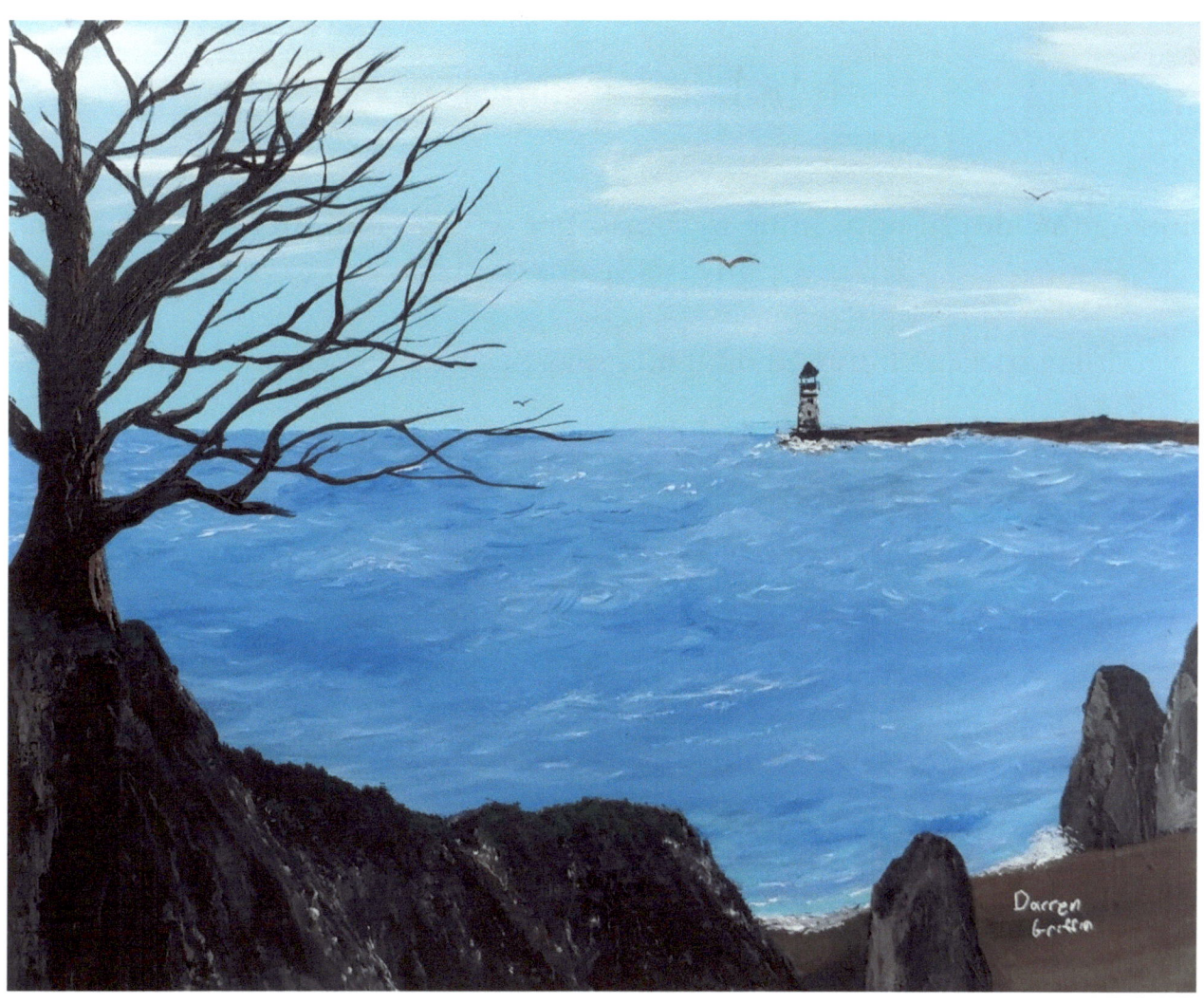

My First Palm Tree

Liking the idea of populating my seascapes with a bit of life, I tried painting my first palm tree.

I like the way it turned out and it has become one of my favorites.

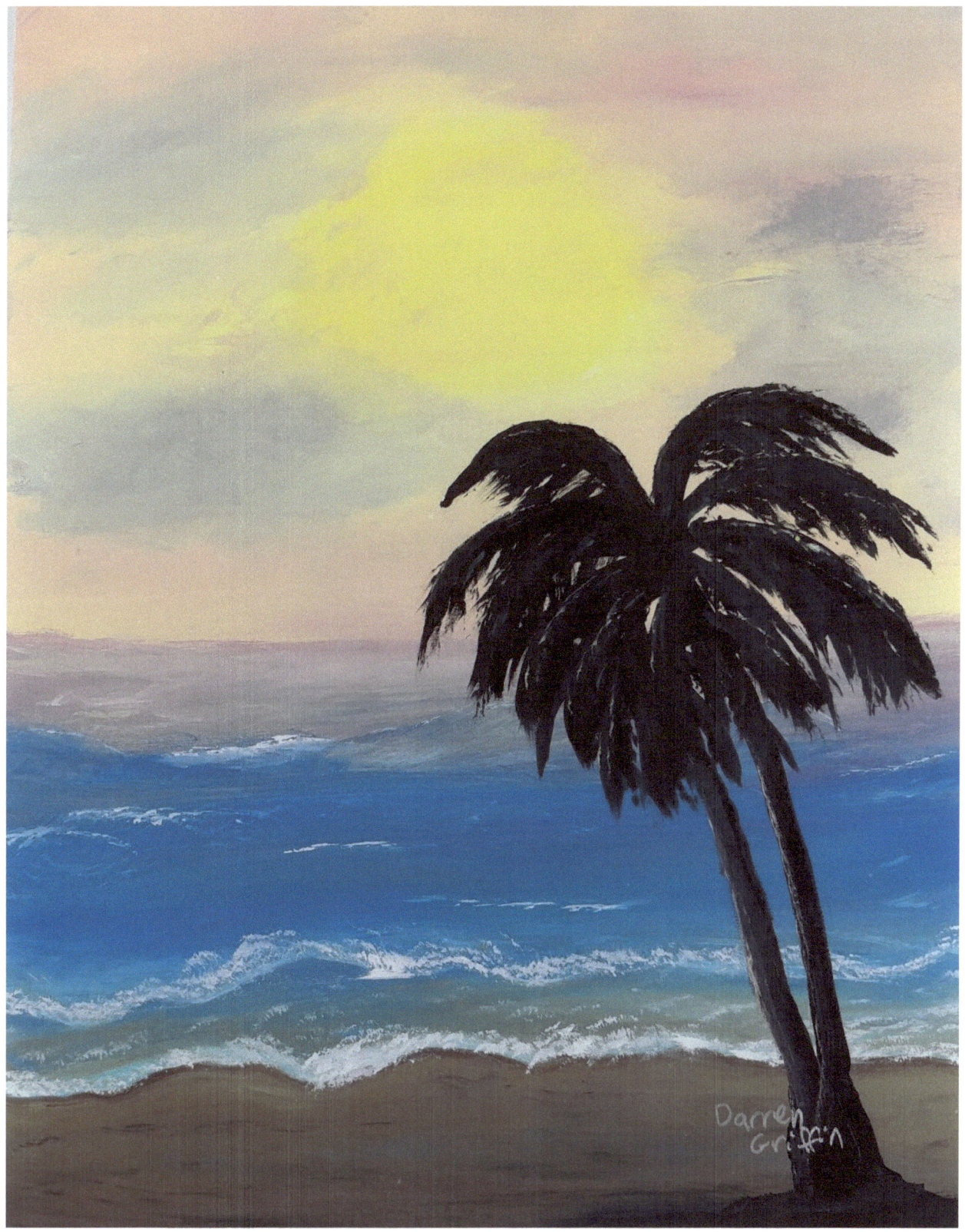

An Experiment

For Christmas my wife gave me four small canvases. I thought it would be interesting to do a 'window pane' type of effect.

I also tried a little boat for the first time.

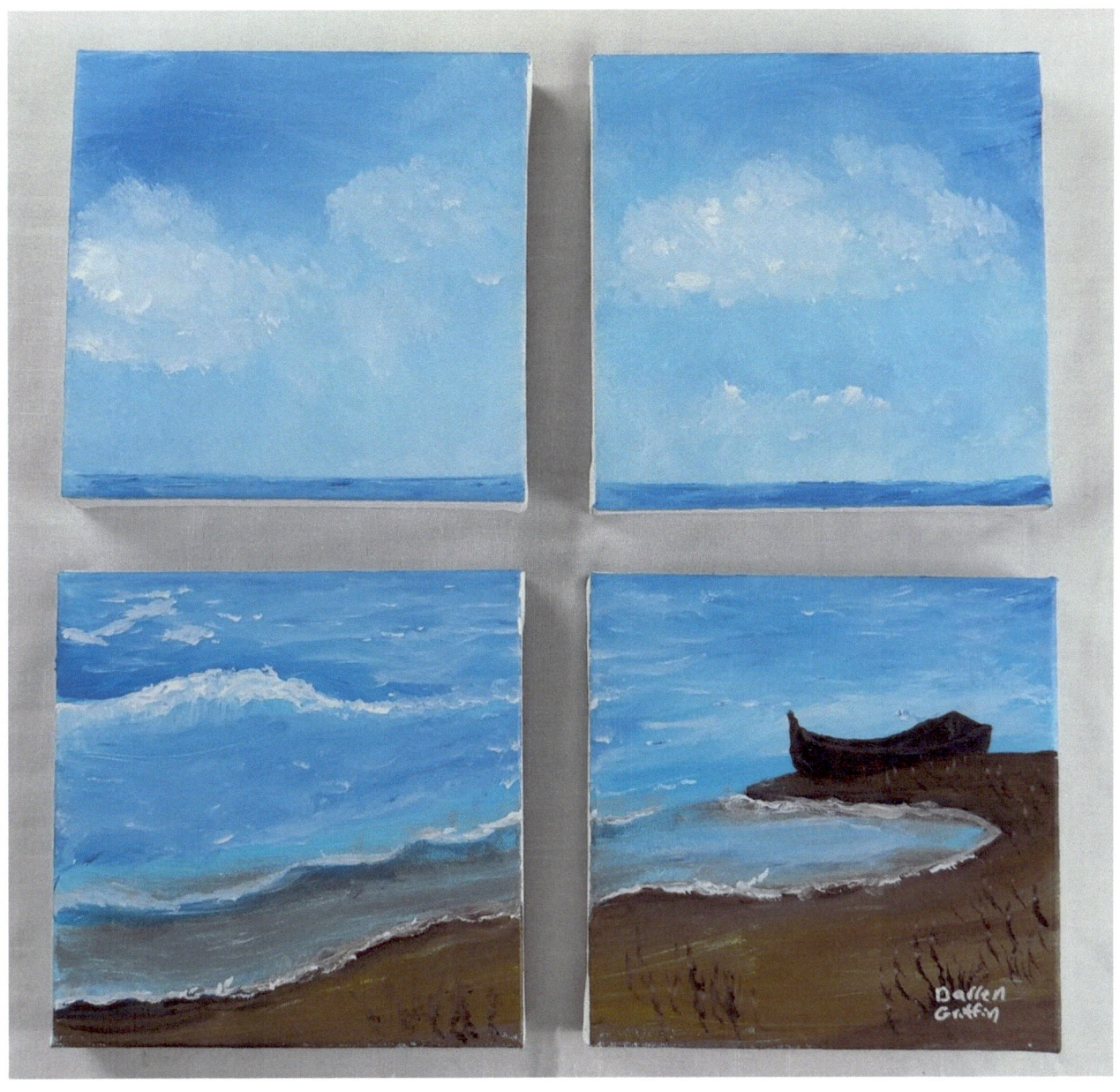

Moonlight

Thus far I had done primarily daytime pieces. I resolved to try a nighttime scene.

I painted the canvas in black. While it was still wet I covered it in dark blue and allowed the blue and black to mix in varying degrees. Layers of white gave me the moonlight. Once again I used a palette knife to do the cliffs.

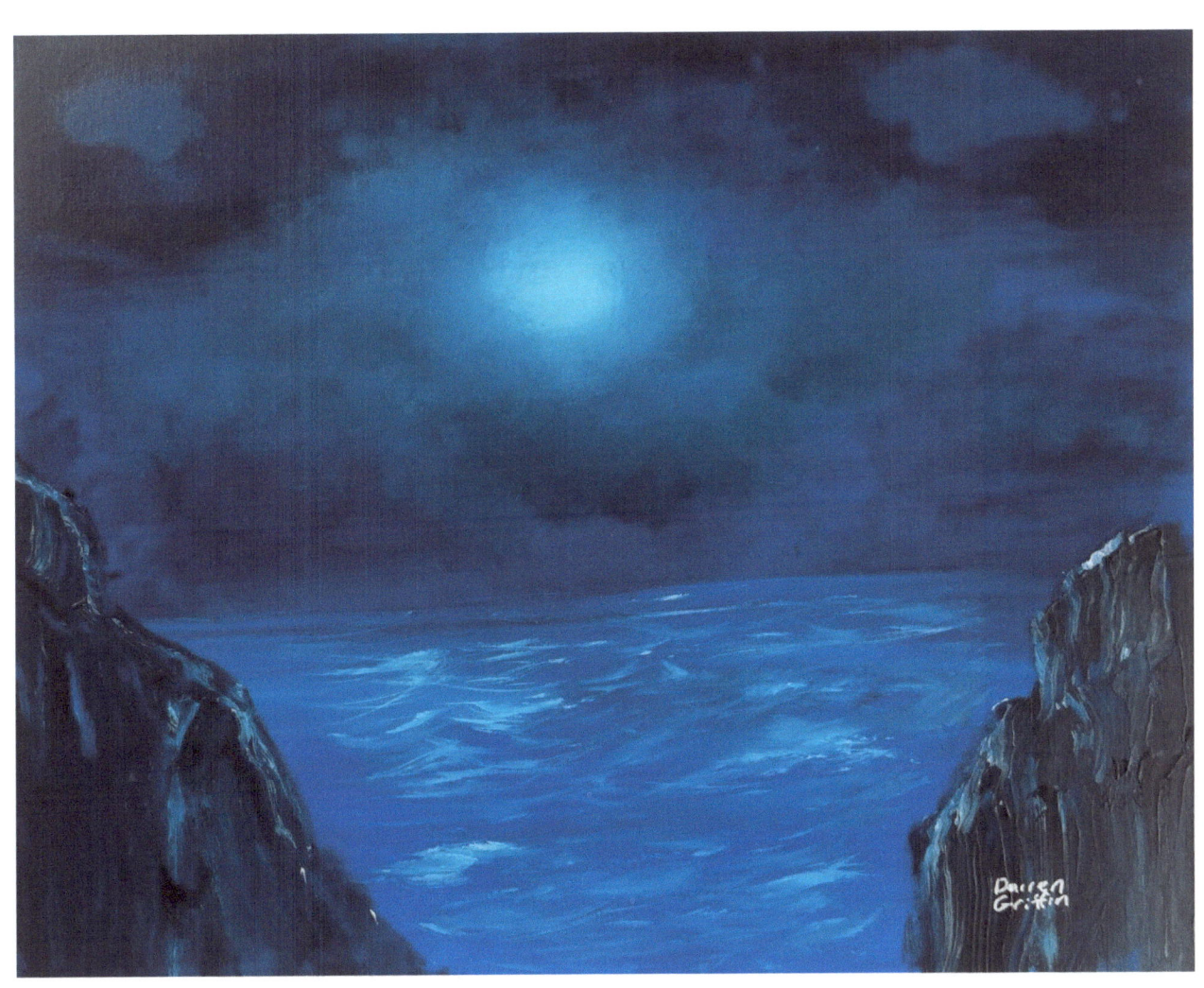

More Moonlight

Liking the results I got with my first moonlight piece I tried a second one, this time including larger waves and well as reflections in the shallow water. My children have pointed out a ghostly figure standing at the foot of the cliff. Didn't do it on purpose.

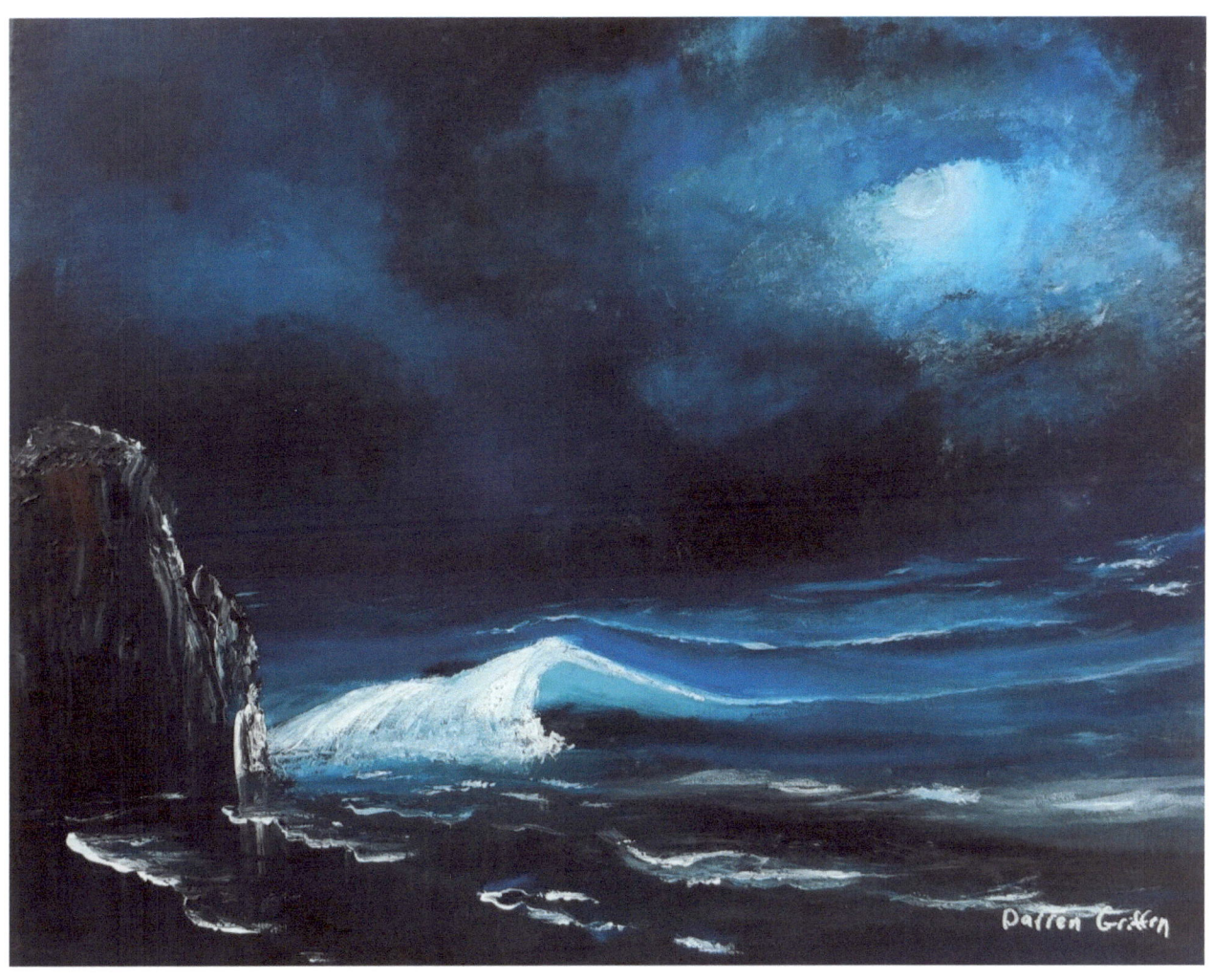

Landscapes

Mountains with a Lake and Cabin

Apparently the secret to a good landscape is learning to use the palette knife to form the mountains and a fan brush to make the trees. It looks so easy on the internet.

After many failed attempts I produced this.

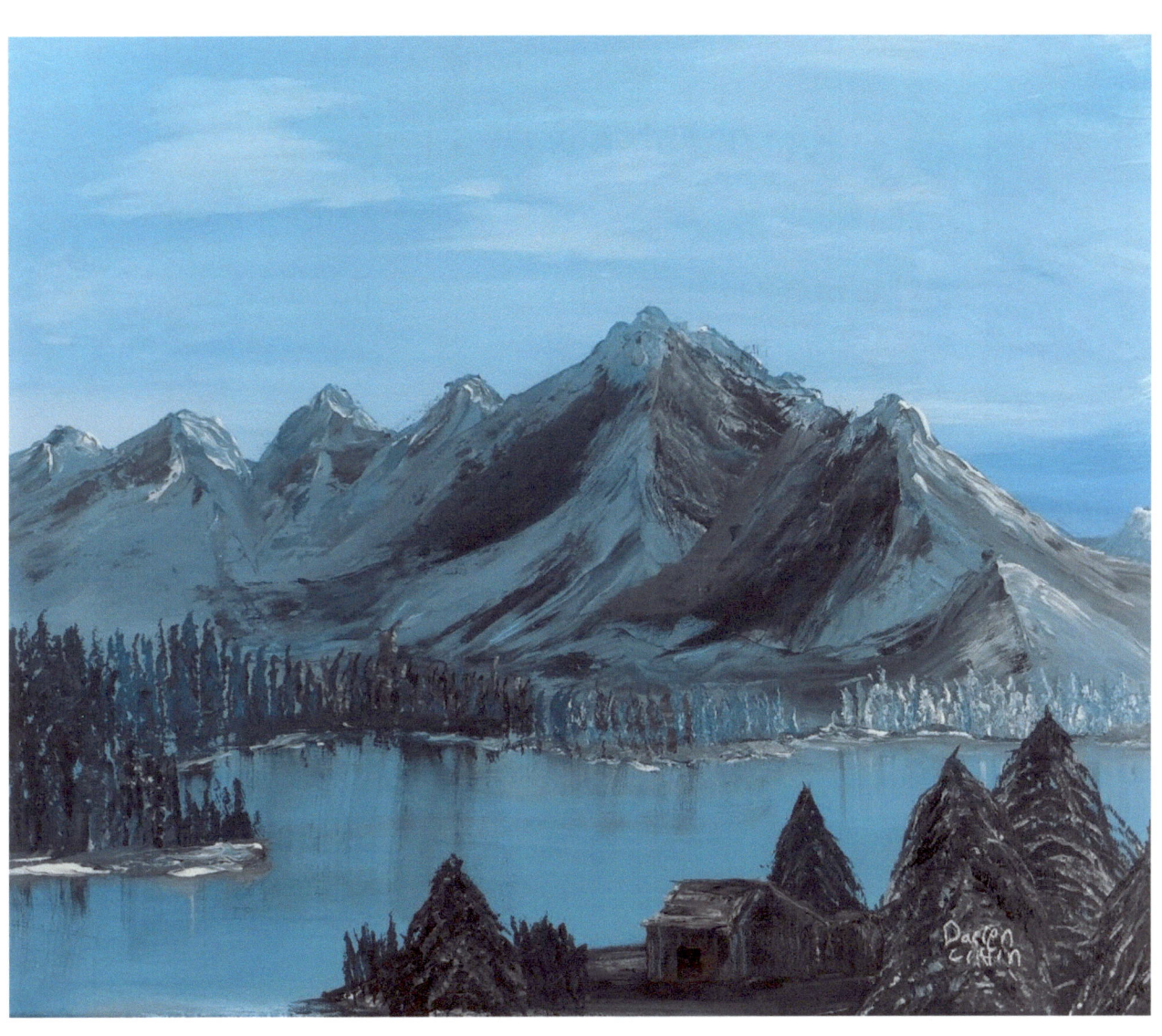

Mountains with a Lake

One of my next attempts. No cabin this time.

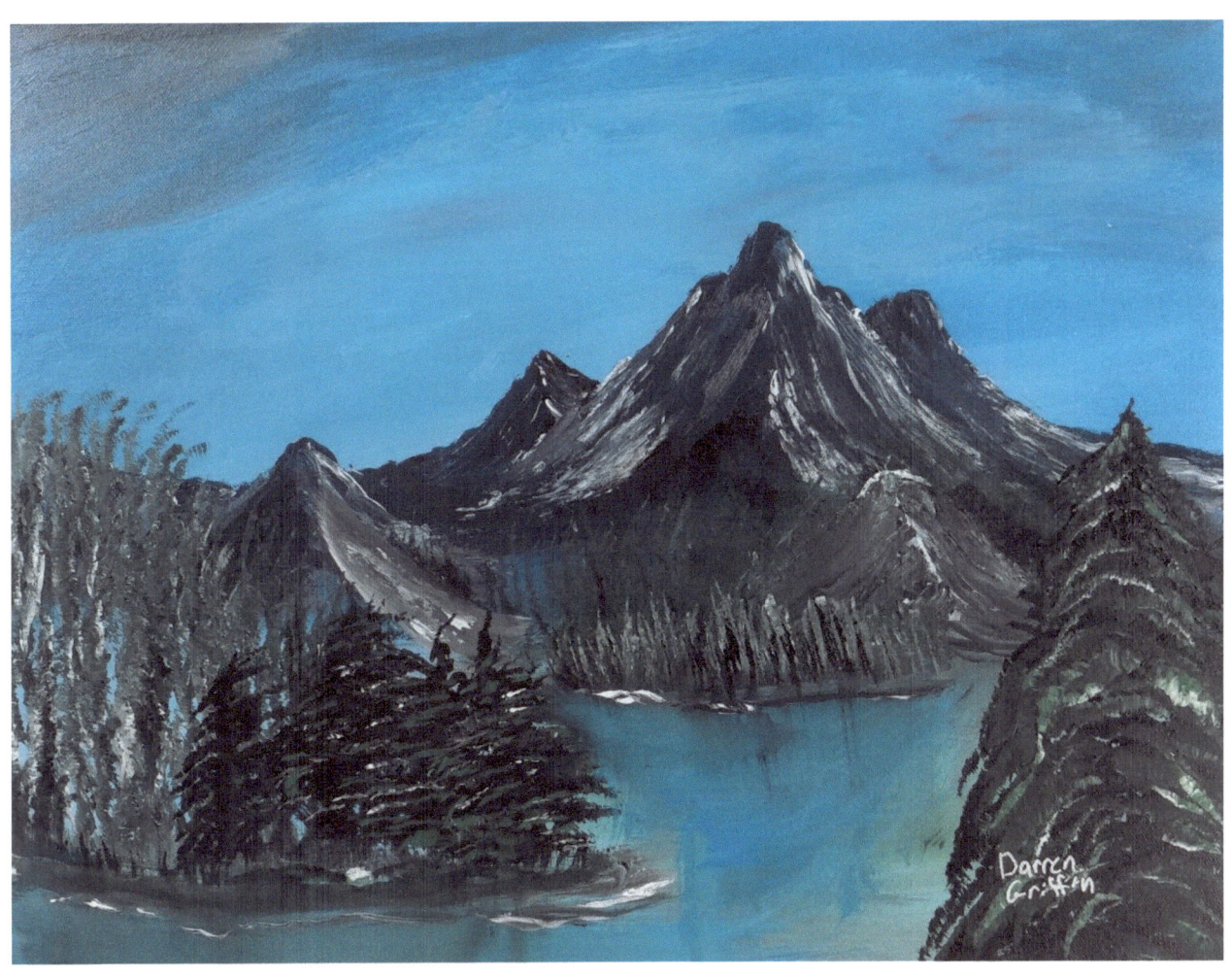

Mountains with Trees

No water in this one. Just mountains and trees.

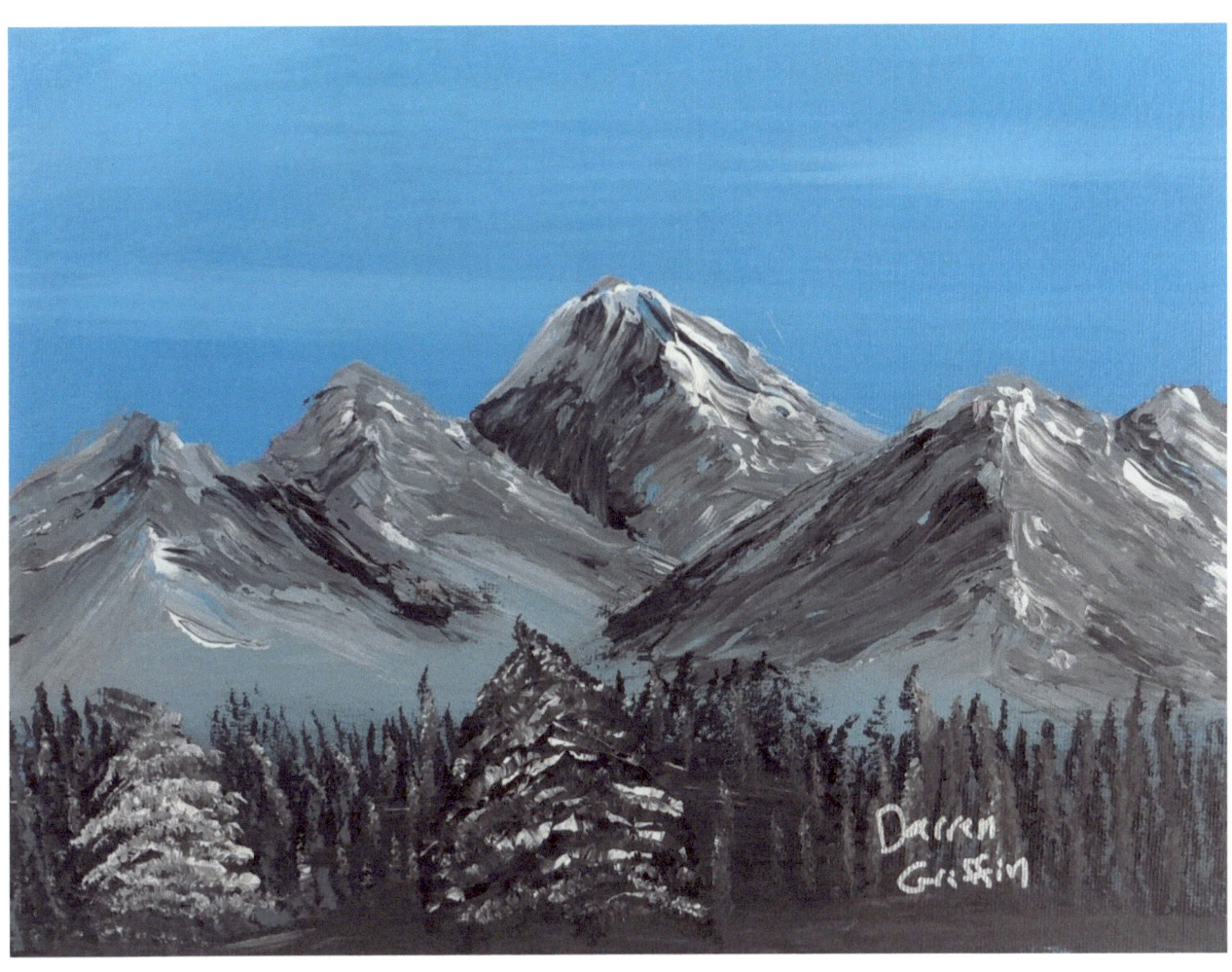

Mountains, Trees and a River

The palette knife is slowly becoming my friend. It's a very effective way to do mountains.

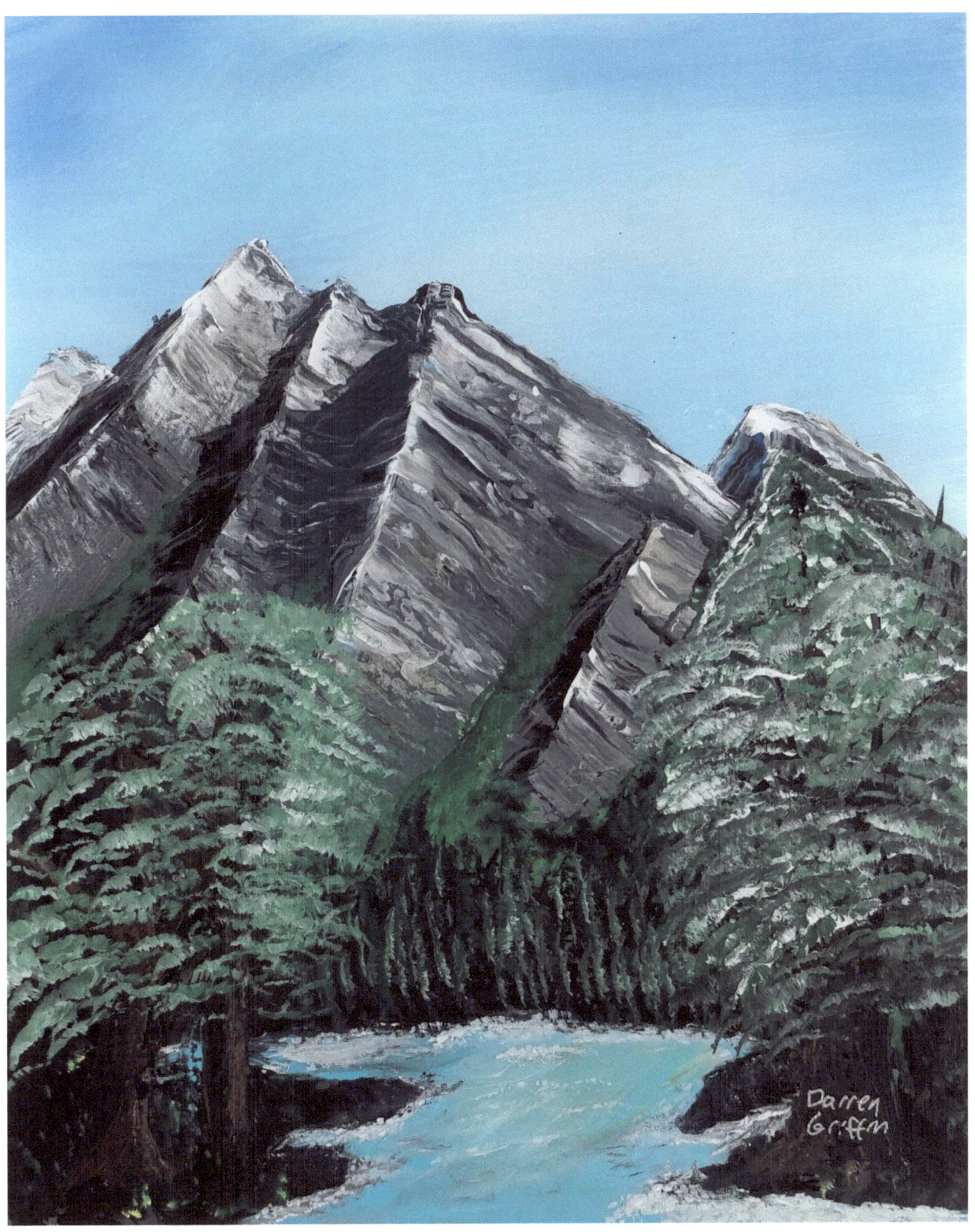

Sunset in Arizona

I spent some time traveling through Arizona back in 2016. This is only the second piece I have done based off of a picture I had taken.

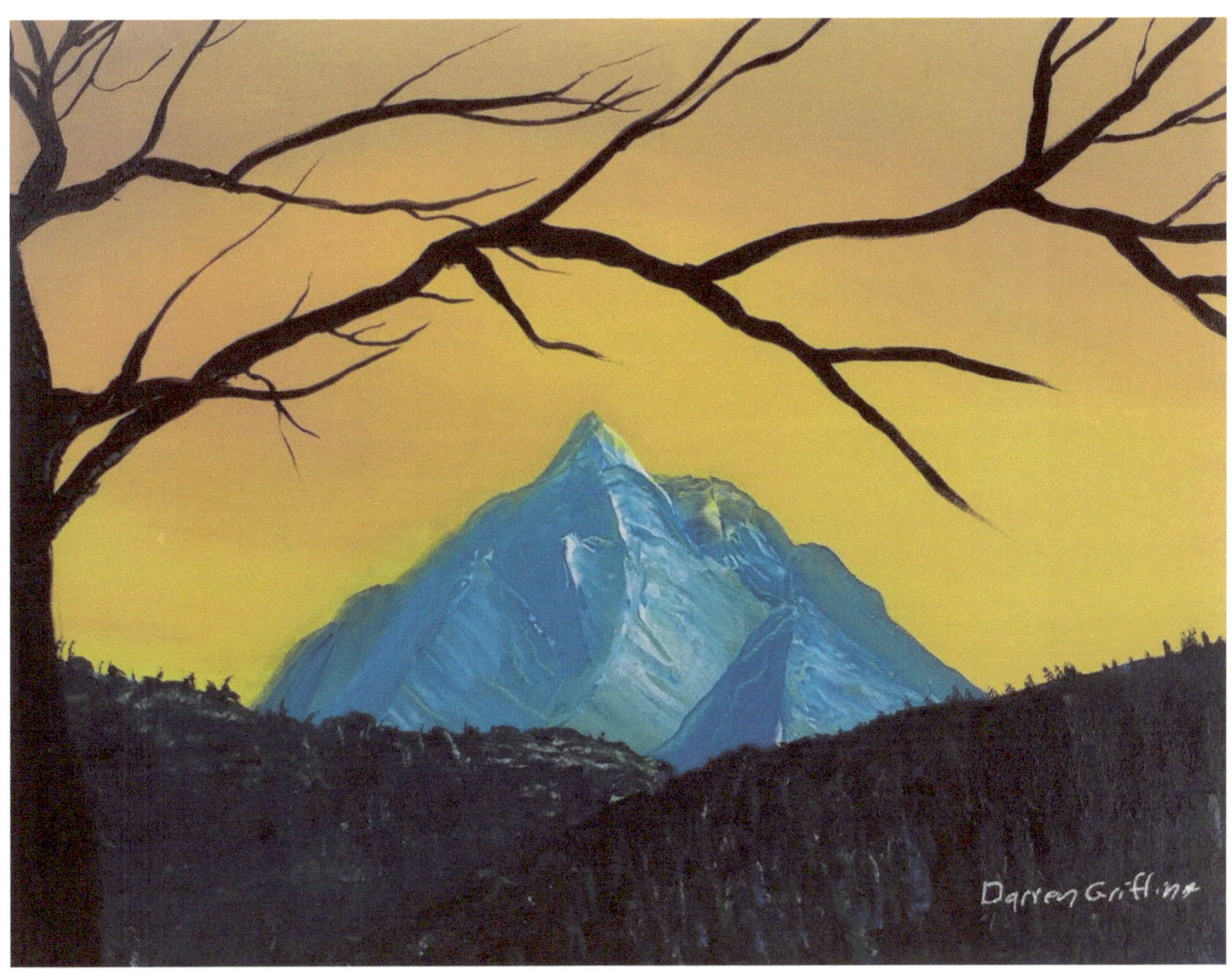

A Little Different Coloring

I noticed most of my landscapes have very similar color palettes, so I resolved to try something new.

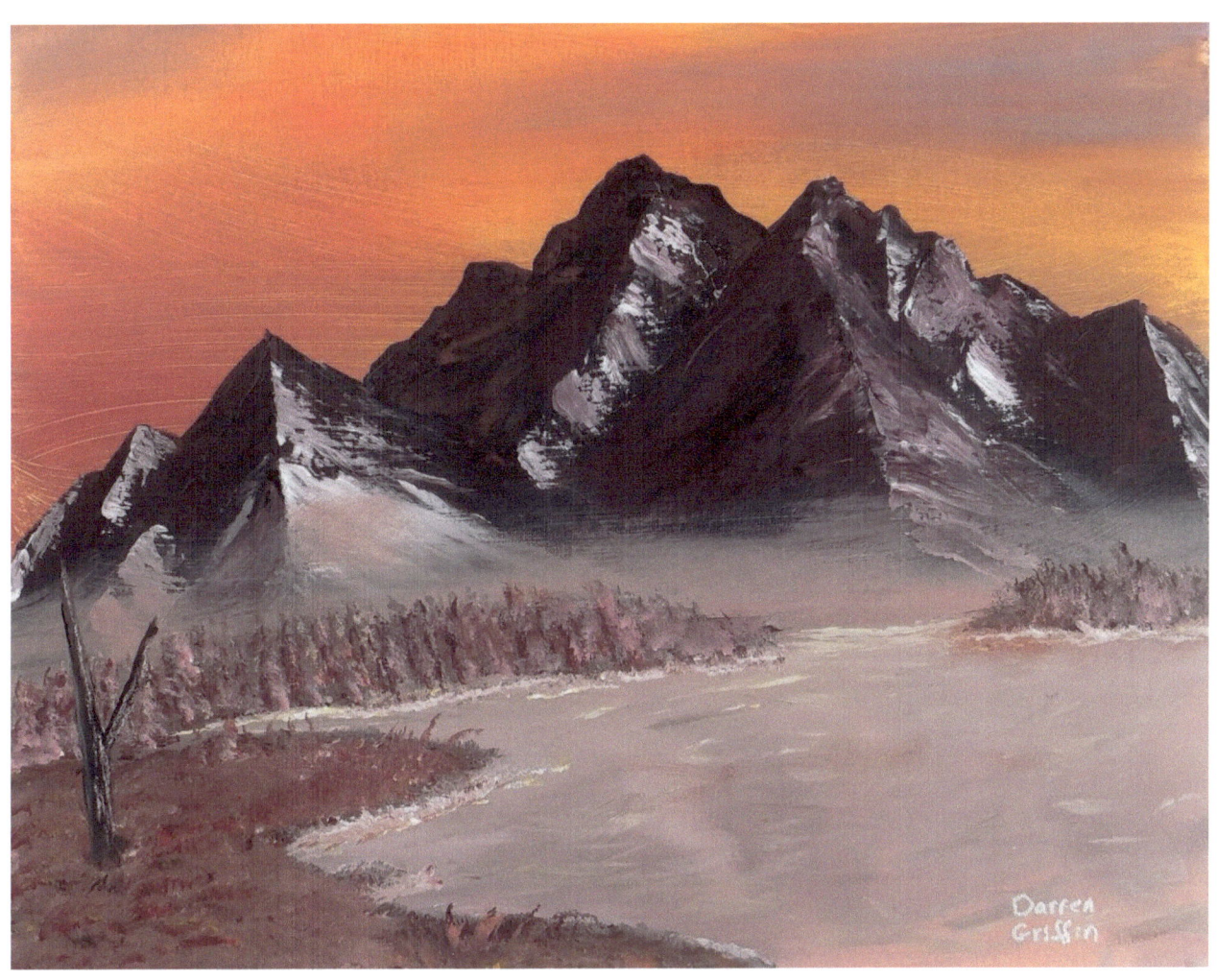

This and That

Christmas

One morning in December of 2017 I woke up and had a picture in my head. It was of the manger with the star shining brightly.

I was able to get it on canvas and I feel it's even better that what I originally pictured.

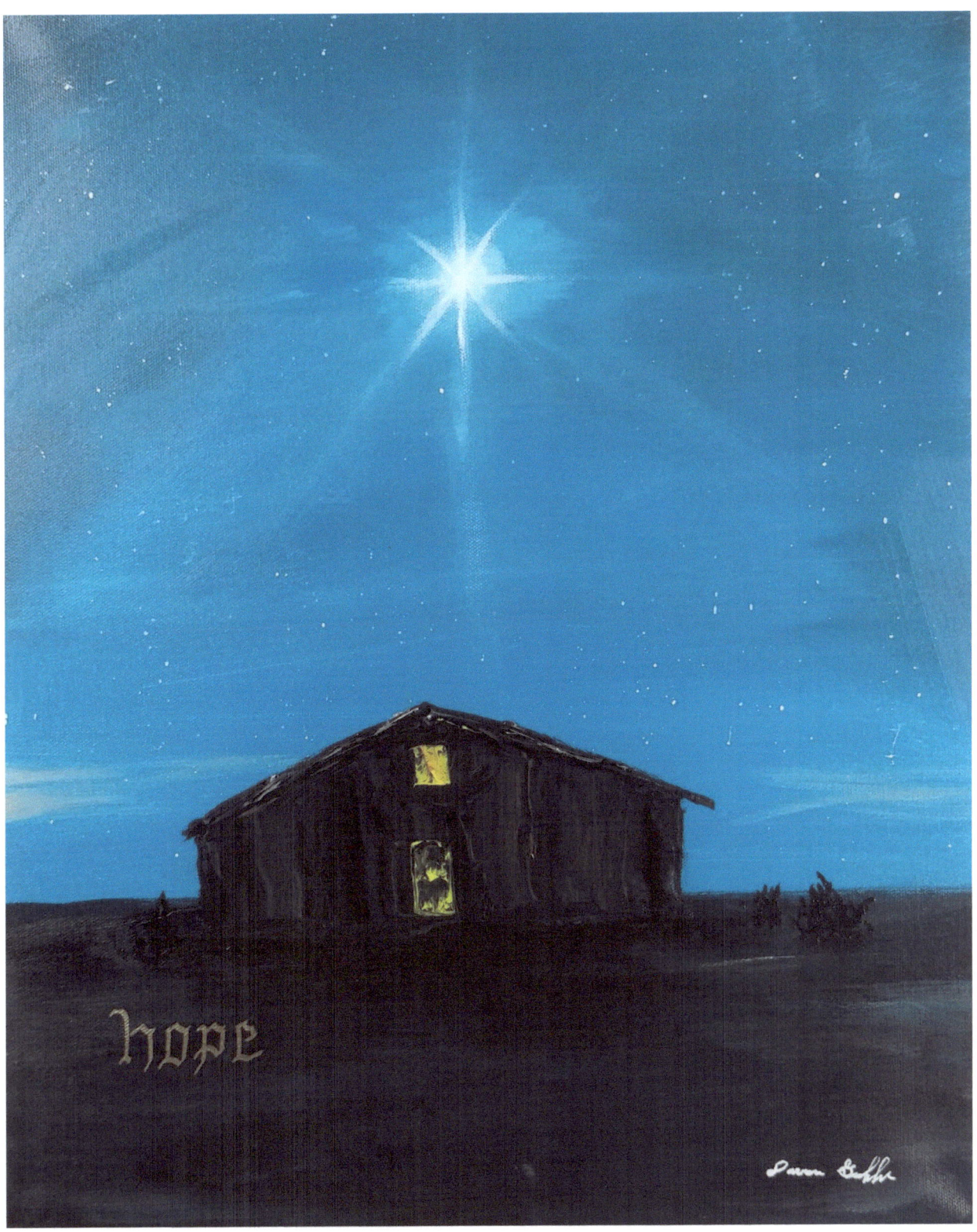

Tree

I decided to branch out (pardon the pun) and try focusing on trees. I found them difficult in the past and wanted to take another shot.

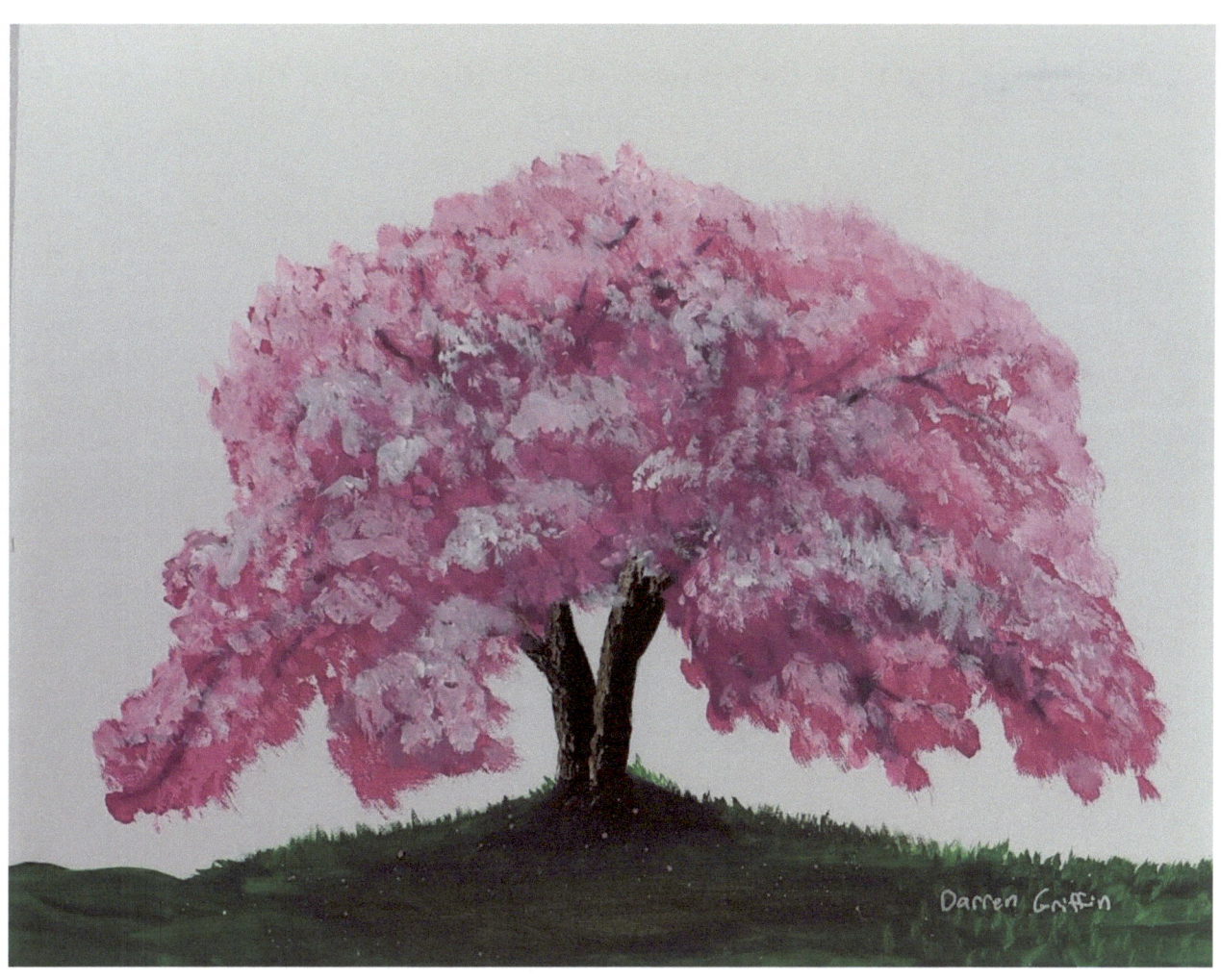

Trees in the Moonlight

I decided to focus on the texture of the bark, so I put the next trees in moonlight.

It turned out with a very Halloweenish look

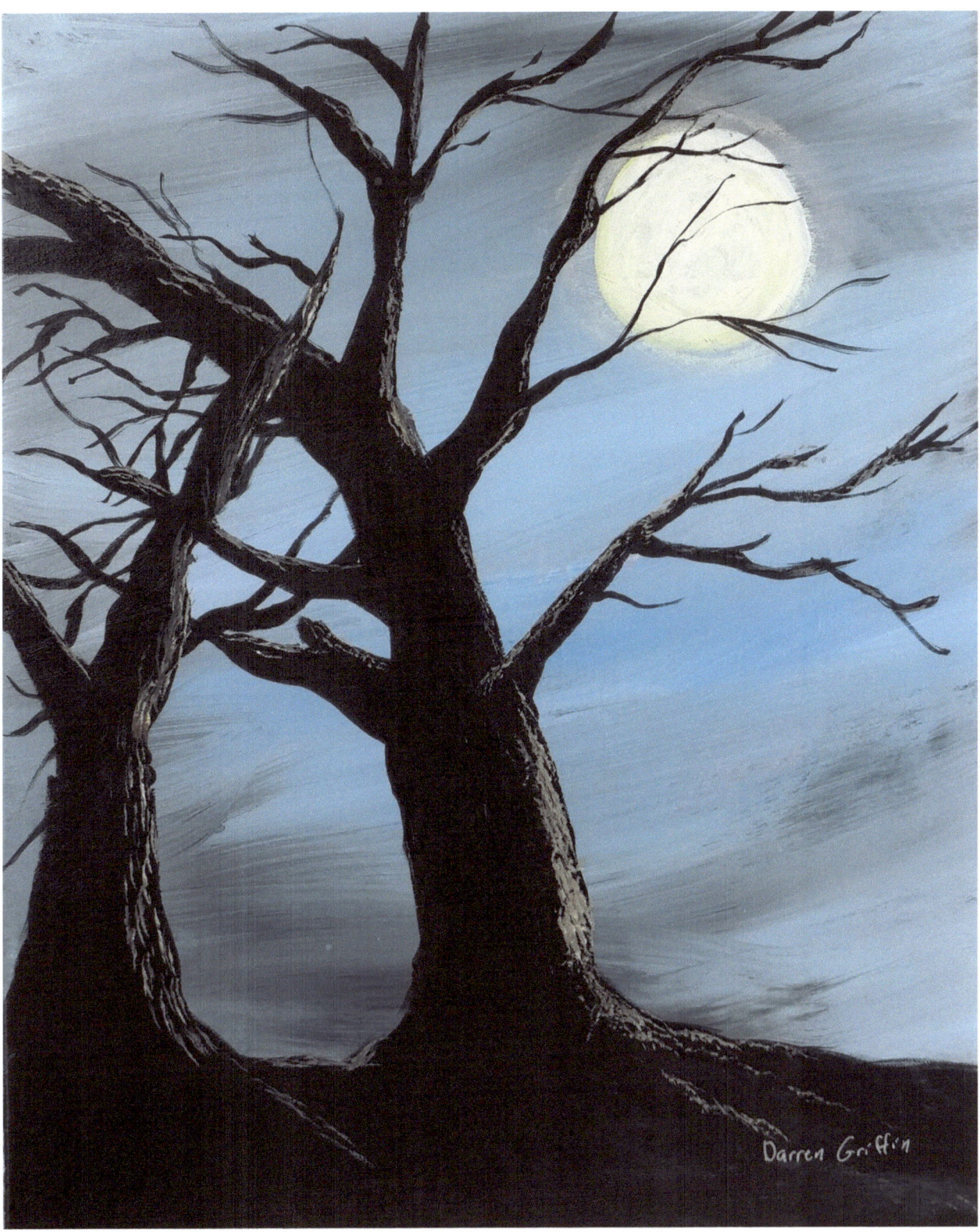

Trees with Water

This has a very tranquil feeling to me. The center is supposed to be trees in the distance as seen through mist, but I think they look more like vines or something.

Oh well, doesn't matter.

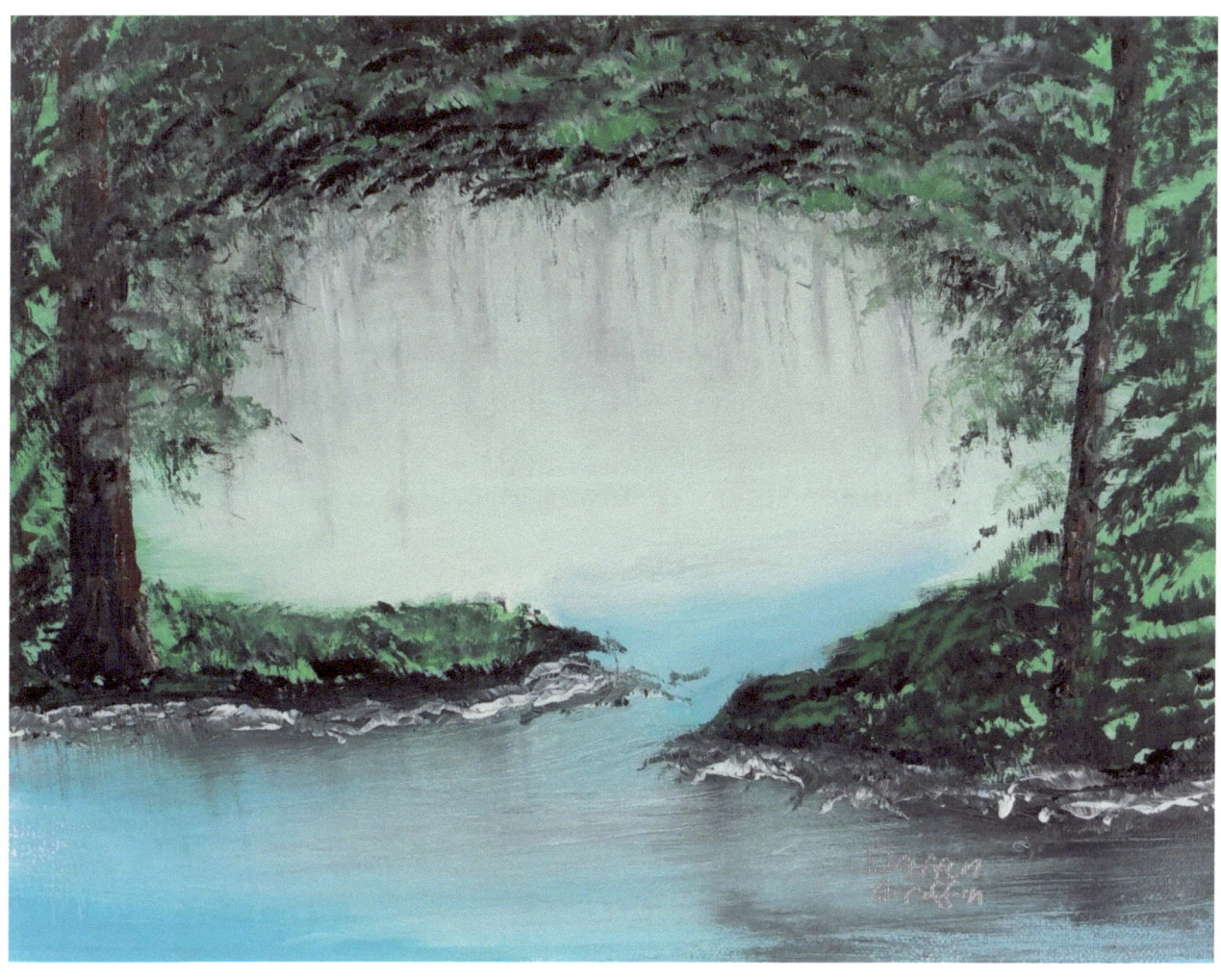

Lightning as Seen With a Headache

I'm prone to get very bad headaches. I have a condition called trigeminal neuralgia and it's very hard for me to function when I'm having a flare up. This piece is the product of a very bad day.

I find it interesting that my style looks very different.

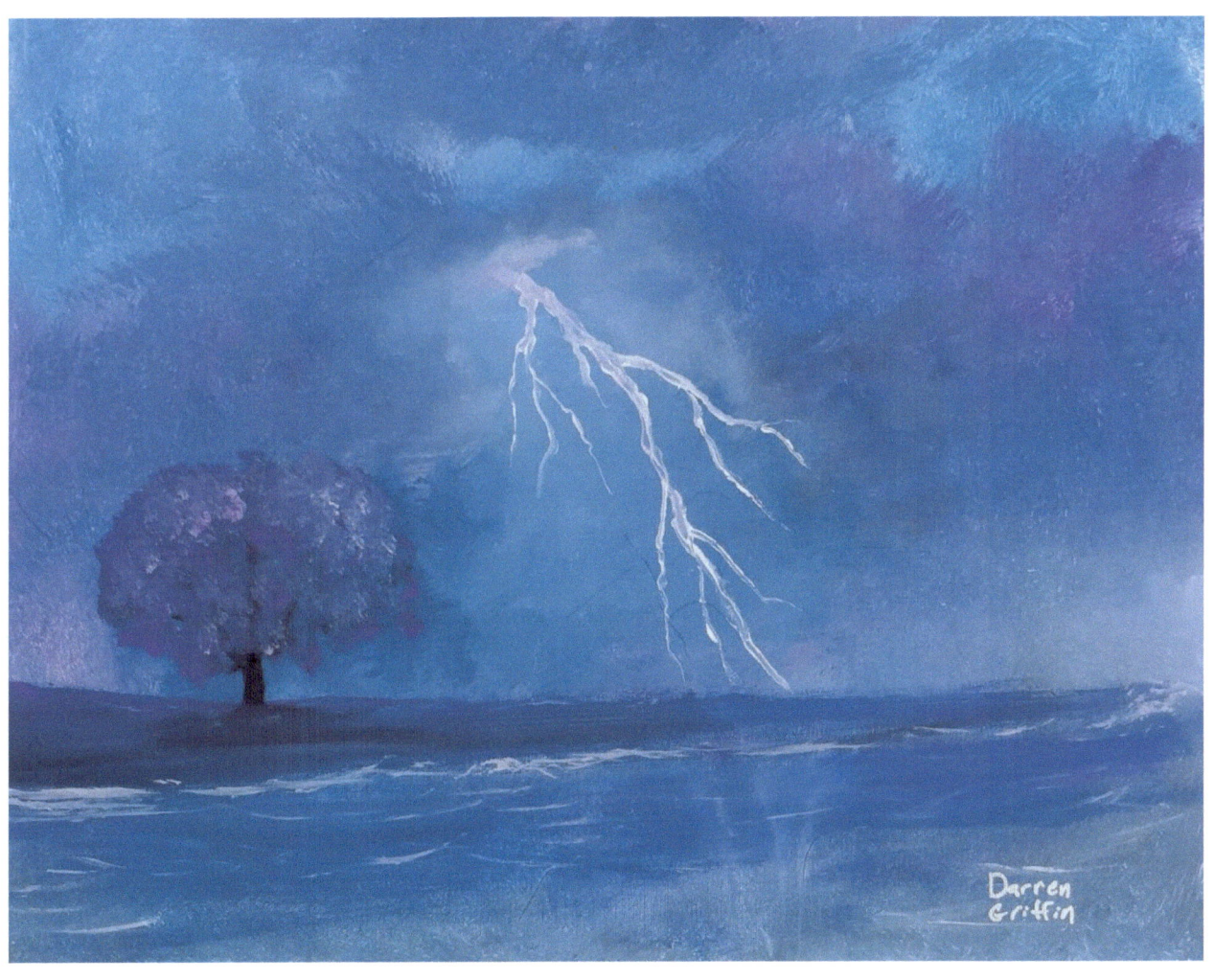

The Bridge

I wanted to do a piece that featured a stone bridge with a great deal of light and shadow to highlight the rocks of which it was made.

I think I got the point across.

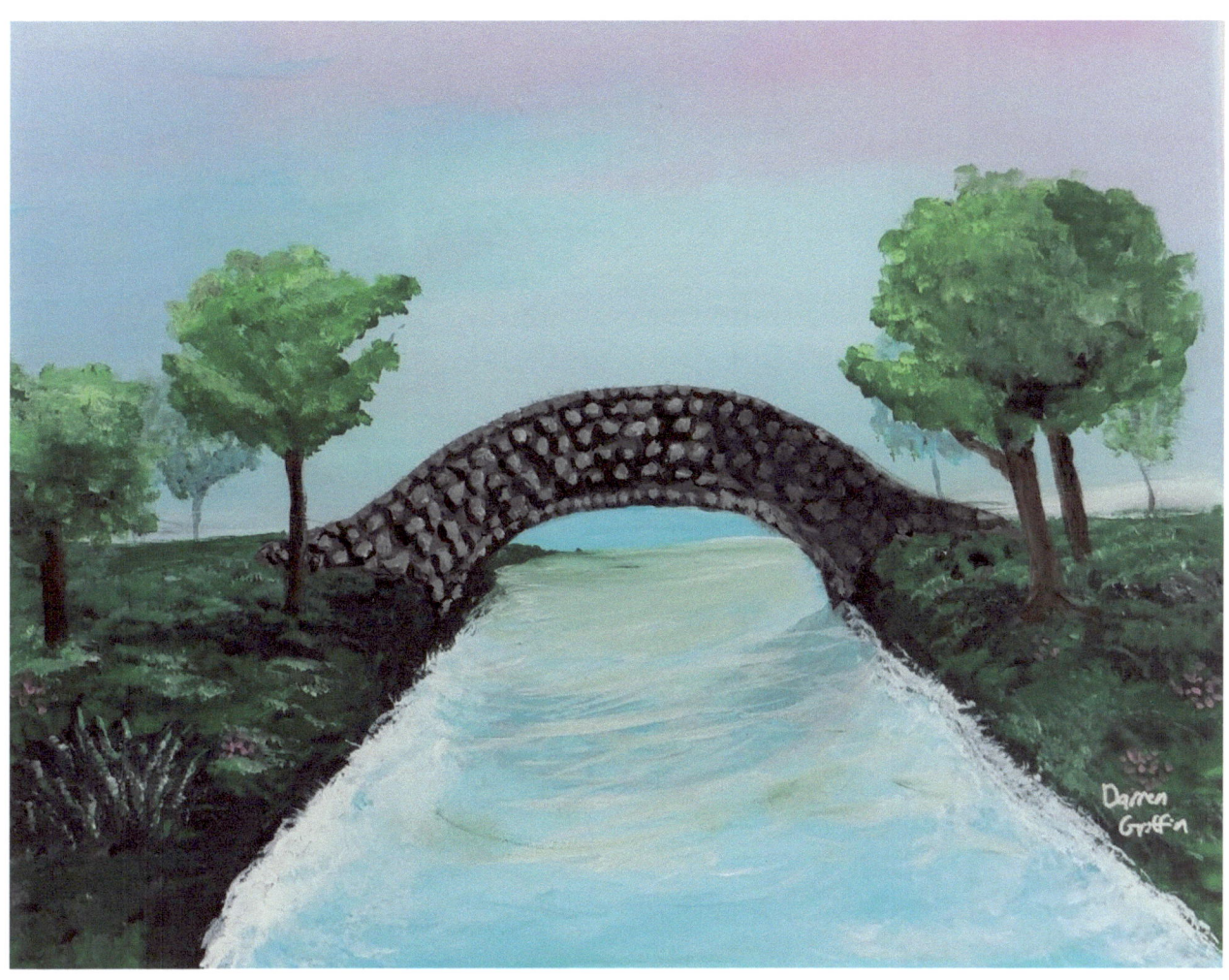

Stars

My daughter Kelly asked me to do a painting of space for her. She said she has memories of her and I sitting and talking on the front porch under the stars.

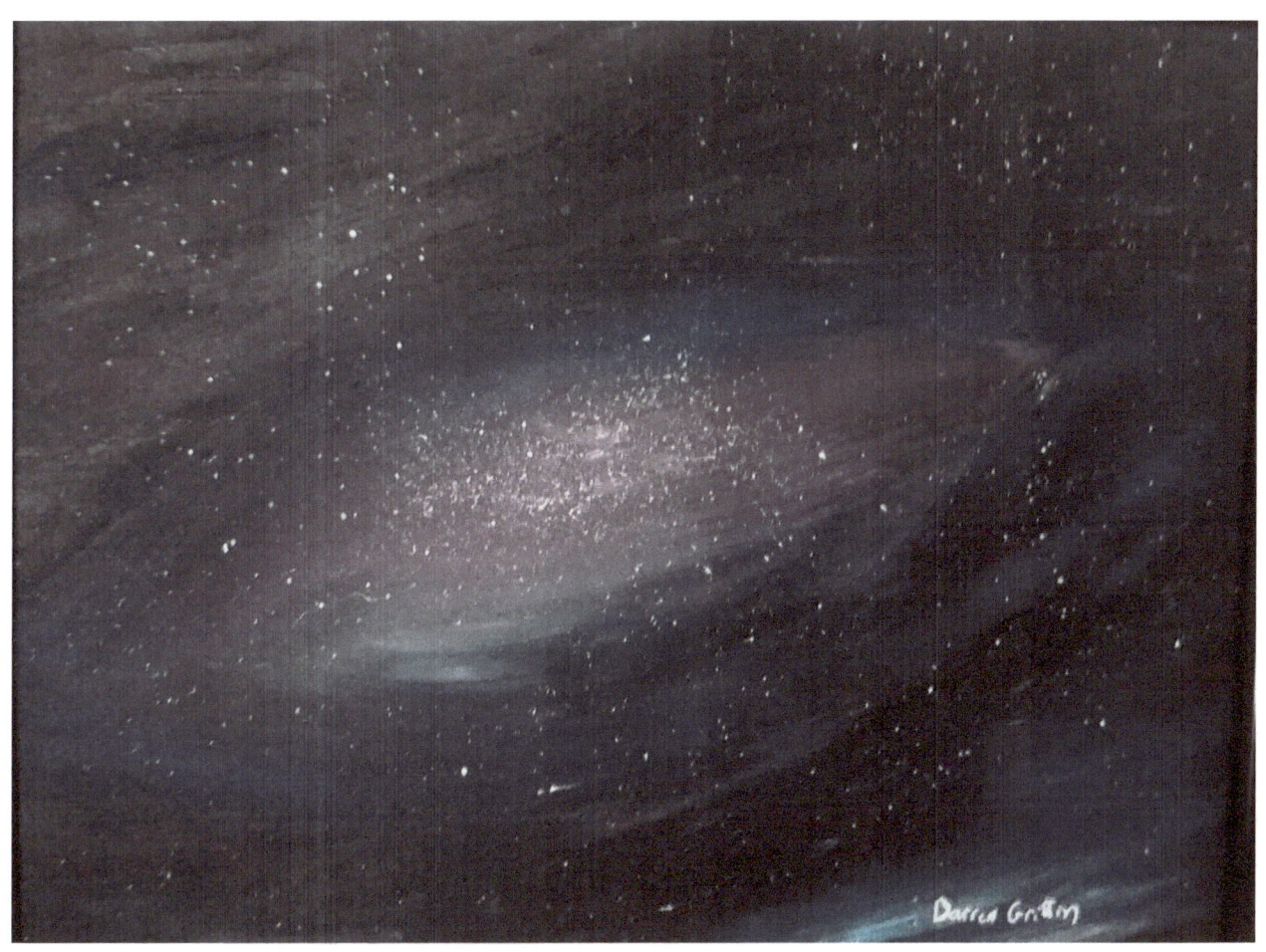

Death of a Child

My oldest daughter, Crystal, lost her first baby. The little girl, Molly, stopped having a heart beat only hours before she was born.

This was devastating to our family.

I learned a lot about grief, mourning, compassion and letting go.

This piece has all of those feelings poured into it.

You'll notice one of the mourners is looking up, as if somehow aware of the little girls state. That's Grandpa. Me.

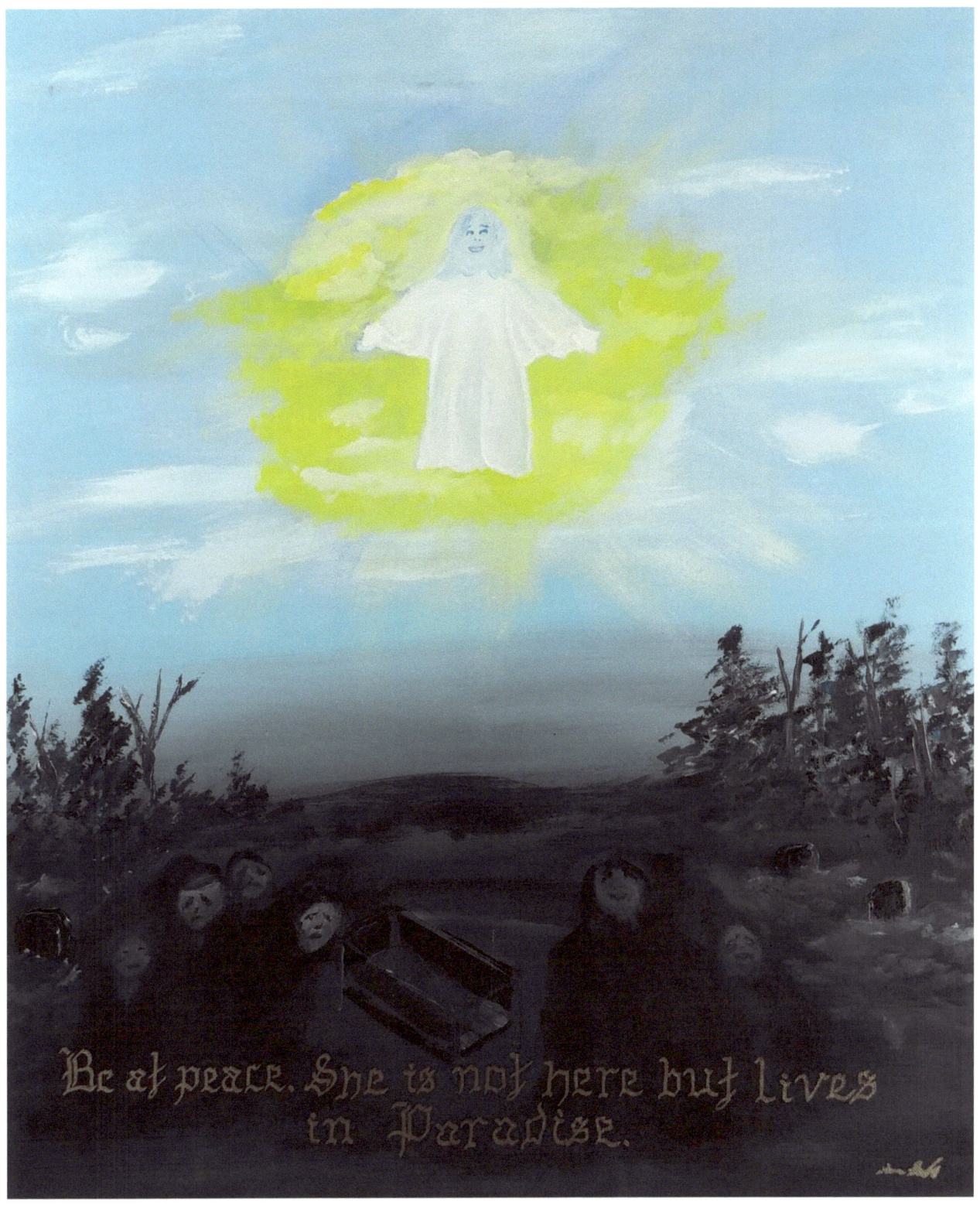

ABOUT THE AUTHOR

Darren Griffin Phd, cs is an internationally known author, key note speaker and composer.

He is a Consulting Hypnotist and teaches a variety of self-help seminars and workshops. His specialties include Stress Management, Self Esteem and Eliminating the Fear of Success, Reiki, Smoking Cessation, Regression, Imprint Removal, Emergency Hypnosis, Pain Management and Forensic Hypnosis.

Darren has also been a ventriloquist since the age of eight. He now has fourteen characters and does shows all over the western United States.

He spent twenty two years in broadcasting and won six EMMYs, seven TELLYs and over twenty awards from the Utah Broadcaster's Association.

He lives in the Western United States with his new wife, seven children, and eight grandchildren.

Feel free to contact him at www.griffintalent.com.